Sixteen Sisters

Retold by Anne Fine
Series Advisor Professor Kimberley Reynolds
Illustrated by Kate Aldous

OXFORD
UNIVERSITY PRESS

Letter from the Author

It's not surprising that my favourite
fairy tales are all about sisters.
When Sue, my elder sister, was
five, and I was three, our parents
decided to have one last baby.
They hoped so much that it would
be a boy, but they had triplet girls.
We soon became the sort of family people stop to
talk to in the street. 'Oh, my! Five girls!'

Everyone loves to read about situations and
feelings they share. *The Twelve Dancing Princesses*
made me feel so much more normal. (There may
have been five of us, but there were twelve of
them!) *Diamonds and Toads* deals with the uglier
feelings of spite and jealousy. And *Snow White
and Rose Red* shows how, even if sisters are very,
very different from one another, they can still be
firm and good friends.

Anne Fine

The Twelve Dancing Princesses

Not all that long ago and not all that far away, there was a country ruled by an irritable King. If a meal was served even a single minute late, he would rush to the kitchens to bellow at the cook. Each time his horse refused to jump a hedge or stream, he'd shake his fist at the heavens. And whenever his wife scolded him for losing his temper in this foolish fashion, the King would fall into a giant sulk and stay sullen all day.

The King and Queen had twelve daughters, born year by year by year. The sisters played together, explored the dark places in the old palace together, and did their homework all at the same time, sitting around a great table.

And because they were princesses as well as sisters, they had to learn to dance, and they did that together too, in the great palace ballroom.

The dancing teacher came in twice a week. He taught them every dance he knew, and they practised the steps over and over till even the youngest and smallest knew each dance perfectly. But still they begged for more.

'Please!' said the eldest to the dancing teacher. 'Don't go home yet!'

'No, not yet!' echoed the sister beside her. 'Just one more dance!'

The twelve girls pleaded with him, all along the line. 'We really don't want to stop yet.' 'We're not tired.' 'We all love dancing.' 'You make it such fun!' 'I'm sure I need more practice.' 'Can't you stay just one more short half hour?' 'Yes, do.' 'Please! Pretty please!' 'We'll be so good.' 'Oh, yes. We will! We will!' 'Oh, please!' 'Please!'

So the poor man would stay for just one more short half hour. Then another. Then another. And in one of the dim and dusty rooms up in the palace attics, the royal cobblers worked around the clock to make enough new dancing shoes for all twelve princesses.

Each week, the Queen sat down to keep the royal accounts. On every Tuesday morning, she would go to her desk to sift through the bills. One day, when he was bored with everyone and everything, the King wandered in and spotted a sheet of paper that the Queen had just put on top of the heap of payments to be made.

'What's this?' he said, waving the quite enormous bill in his wife's face. 'All of this money for new shoes? What is going on?'

'It's the dancing,' the Queen said. 'Our darling daughters spend so many hours in the ballroom that they wear through their shoes as if they were made of paper.'

The King flew into one of his tempers. 'This has to stop!' he bellowed, and stormed along the palace corridor until he reached the ballroom. 'Listen to me, girls!' he shouted. 'These shoe bills are beyond a joke! From now on, it's bare feet for everyone!'

His daughters simply giggled, kicked off their shoes and danced as well and happily as they'd done before.

To
His Majesty the King ~
owing for 24 new pairs
of Dance Slippers.

48 Gold Coins

ROYAL
SHOE MAKER

To
His Majesty the King ~
owing for 12 new pairs
of Dance Slippers.

24 Gold Coins

ROYAL
SHOE MAKER

On went the lessons, week by week. Every few days, the King popped his head round the door to make sure his twelve dancing daughters weren't back in their shoes and costing him more money.

But still the bills came in.

The King was mystified. He waved the new bills at the Queen. 'What's going on? Our girls dance in bare feet. How can they still be getting through so many pairs of shoes?'

The Queen sighed. 'I'll ask the nannies.'

But the nannies shook their heads. 'We can't explain it,' they admitted to the Queen. 'Each night, we tell your daughters to lay their shoes together neatly at the ends of their beds. And in the morning they are worn to ribbons. You'd think the girls had put them on again and danced all night.'

When the Queen told the King, he grew even crosser than he'd been before. 'Send for the princesses! At once!'

Soon all the sisters stood in front of him. Some kept their faces straight, but others couldn't stop their giggling, and that made the King even more angry.

'You tell me what is going on,' he warned, 'or you'll regret it! Your nannies say you go to bed each night, but every morning your shoes are worn to shreds. How does that happen?'

'Say nothing,' murmured the eldest sister, and the whisper ran along the line.
'Say nothing.'

'Say nothing.'

'Say nothing ... '

'Say nothing ... '

The King sat waiting. When no answer came, he lost his temper entirely. 'That's it!' he stormed. 'I am a reasonable man, but you've pushed me too far. I'm going to offer a reward to the first person who can tell me why your shoes are worn out every morning after you've been in bed all night.'

The Queen, who had the royal accounts in mind, looked rather worried. 'What *sort* of a reward?' she asked her husband. 'With all these shoe bills coming in, we have no extra money for rewards.'

The King looked all along the line of silent daughters. He noticed for the first time that his eldest girl had grown as tall as him. And she had a smile on her face. Somehow that made him even more furious. 'Right, then!' he declared. 'If we can't afford a proper reward, then I'll invite every rich prince I know to come and try to solve the mystery. And the first one to tell us how this strange thing happens may marry any one of you twelve girls who is as tall as I am.'

'But that's just *me*,' the eldest daughter said.

'Your choice,' the King said sulkily. 'All that you have to do to put a stop to this is tell me how your shoes get ruined every night.'

At this, his eldest daughter smiled even more broadly. 'I'll wait and see how handsome the princes are first,' she said, and she and her sisters stood giggling until their father sent them out of his sight, back to the nannies.

* * *

Next day, the proclamation was sent far and wide, and one by one over the next few weeks, all manner of princes came. Each spent a whole day in the princesses' company. They'd watch the dancing lessons, and chat to the nannies, and eat lunch with the sisters. In the afternoons, they'd go for walks with the King's daughters if the weather was fine, or play board games if the weather was awful. The eldest princess took particular interest in whether she liked the look of them, and whether they could make her laugh, and if they played chess well enough to give her a good game. (But, as the nannies whispered to one another, you couldn't blame a girl for wanting to get to know a prince whom she might end up having to marry.)

Each evening, a camp bed was put up outside the great long bedroom that the princesses shared, and all the sisters said goodnight politely to the prince of the day as they went past. Then, as soon as the nannies had clumped off downstairs to get their own supper, the eldest sister slipped out of the bedroom carrying a tray with a small jug of some strange red cordial that smelled deliciously of herbs, and four crisp biscuits.

'This is for you,' she'd say.

She'd perch on the nearby chair, chatting away to the prince and watching carefully as he drank the rich red cordial and ate the biscuits. The moment she could see that he was yawning and his eyes were drooping fast, she'd say goodnight again and curtsy one last time before she went back to her sisters in the bedroom and shut the door.

In the morning, each prince had woken murmuring, 'Oh, fiddlesticks! I truly meant to stay awake all night to see if the princesses left their room.' Then he would cheer himself. 'But what a good night's sleep I had! So deep! So refreshing!' And in this way the weeks drifted past. Not one of the princes heard a sound. Not one of them saw anything odd. But when the nannies came upstairs, they'd find that the princesses' shoes were worn to shreds, as usual.

At that, each prince in turn was ordered off. 'Useless!' the King would mutter. 'Worse than the nannies!'

And, 'Not quite up to scratch,' would

murmur the eldest daughter. And so the whisper ran along the line. 'That prince was not quite up to scratch.'

'Not up to scratch.'

'Not up to scratch ... '

'Not up to scratch ... '

The sisters would all giggle. Then they would hurry off to dancing class, happily forgetting all about princes until the next arrived to try his luck.

* * *

The months went by, and soon every land around had plain run out of princes. The Queen kept sighing over the shoemakers' bills. The King never failed to pop his head around the ballroom door to make sure his daughters danced barefoot. The nannies checked the girls' shoes every night, and were astonished each morning to find them all worn useless, paper thin.

The King sent for his eldest daughter. 'I'm warning you,' he said. 'This has to stop. Tonight the nannies are going to check your shoes, and if tomorrow morning they're in shreds as usual, I'll put up posters inviting any man in the land to try his luck at solving this mystery.'

The eldest princess gave her father that teasing smile that drove him wild. 'And if some horrid stranger manages, will I still have to marry him?'

'Yes!' the King shouted, in a temper. 'Yes, you will!'

'Even if he has not a sixpence to his name, is ugly as sin, and can't play chess or make me laugh?'

'Yes. Even if he has nothing but the rags he stands in and a face like a camel's. Even if he's too weak in wits to grasp the rules of Snakes and Ladders, and so miserable by nature that he spends the whole of every day moaning and scolding.'

'Oooh!' said the princess. 'This is all getting exciting.' And she went off to warn her sisters, 'Don't grow as tall as I have, or you might end up like me, threatened with marriage to a ragged, stupid, gloomy camel.'

And because the sisters were sure their secret would never be discovered, they ran off laughing to their next dance class.

* * *

A few days later, deep in a forest, a soldier, not in the first bloom of youth, was limping back from the wars. Reaching a clearing, he came across a bent old woman in clothes so ragged and worn, they were almost in tatters.

'Kind soldier,' she begged him, 'spare me a penny so I can buy myself a mouthful of bread.'

The soldier only had two pennies left in all the world. Digging them out of his pocket, he gazed at them sadly for a moment, then handed one to the woman. 'Here,' he said. 'It's half my fortune, but you can have it, and welcome.'

'You are a kind and generous man,' said the old woman, 'and you deserve a better fortune than your last penny.' She pointed to the poster pinned to a tree behind them. 'You should try your luck at solving the King and Queen's mystery.'

Curious, the soldier studied the poster, which said:

Reward

I offer half of my kingdom and my eldest daughter's hand in marriage to any man who can discover how the princesses dance their shoes to ribbons each and every night.

Louis Rex

'Tempting,' the soldier said. 'I could make do with half a sixpence rather than half a kingdom. But I would certainly like a dancing wife.'

The old woman chuckled, then she said to him, 'Because you've been so generous to me, I'll give you something in return. Here, take my cloak.'

The length of tattered cloth she held out to the soldier looked so threadbare and grubby he didn't fancy carrying it about. 'Truly,' he said, pushing it back towards her, 'we hardy old soldiers have learned to keep ourselves warm enough.'

'Take it,' she insisted. 'And you be sure to take good care of it because it's magic. Whenever you wrap it round you, you'll become invisible.'

Indeed I will! the soldier thought to himself. *In this sad covering, I'll just appear as one more beggar in town!* But he did not want to hurt the old lady's feelings since even the poorest soul has their pride. And so he took the grey, old garment that she'd pressed on him, thanked her and said goodbye.

The woman set off down the forest path then turned back one last time. 'Oh, I forgot!' she said. 'Don't eat the biscuits and don't drink the cordial!'

Instantly, she was gone.

The soldier stared at the dark place between the trees where she had vanished then looked at the cloak. He muttered to himself, '"Don't eat the biscuits!" When did a man as poor as I last see a biscuit? I can't even remember! As for "Don't drink the cordial!" Why, it's been years since anyone offered me anything other than plain old water drawn from a well.'

He looked at the cloak again. 'And this old rag is sure to be thick with fleas.'

But he knew if he dropped it in the forest, then she might stumble on it some day soon as she walked past. So, sighing, he tucked the horrid thing under his arm and as he kept on down the path, he almost forgot about it.

Reaching the edge of the forest, he stepped out from between the trees into a sharp wind. The soldier shivered. First, he dropped the cloak to rub his chilled arms to warm them, then he looked at it more closely. 'At least it's made of wool. It might be hopping with fleas, but it will still be warm.'

The soldier wrapped the cloak around his shoulders. At once, his whole body disappeared from sight. He tore the cloak off. Back his body came in view. He flung the cloak around himself again.

There was no question about it. He was invisible! Even as he was standing there beside the path, his mouth fallen open in shock, two shepherds passed without so much as one short, curious glance in his direction.

'This can't be true!' the soldier told himself, and quickly he ran till he was once again in front of them. He danced and capered in their path. The shepherds paid him not the least attention.

'Right,' said the soldier to himself. 'I will go off and try my luck for this fine dancing wife.'

He reached the palace early the next evening. The Queen took one look at his drab old soldier's uniform and tattered cloak, and rolled her eyes to heaven. The King called in his eldest daughter.

'See?' he said. 'We have run out of handsome, rich young princes. And now this ragged old soldier is here to try his luck.'

'I may be ragged, but I'm not that old,' the soldier said.

Thinking her father had been very rude to someone who had fought his wars for him, the eldest daughter said, 'And I am not that young.' She smiled at the soldier.

'Come with me,' she said. 'We'll offer you a bath and supper then a warm bed outside our room.'

'You're very kind,' the soldier said, and followed the eldest princess up the palace stairs. She told the nannies, 'Here is another man who hopes to win half the kingdom and my hand in marriage. Treat him well.'

The nannies were horrified. 'Give us your uniform,' they said, 'and that extremely grubby cloak, and we will wash them while you sleep.'

'I shan't be sleeping tonight,' the soldier said. 'I'm here to watch to see how it is that the princesses' shoes get worn to ribbons. But when I've solved the mystery, I'll hand you all my grubby clothes, and welcome.'

The nannies tutted and fussed, but there was nothing they could do. The soldier was firm. So in the end, they gave him his fine supper without the bath and set up his bed outside the princesses' bedroom door.

After they'd gone, he lay there in his clothes, with the magic cloak under his pillow. And just as he was thinking about how much he'd liked the eldest sister's graceful way of telling off her father for his bad manners, the door in front of him swung open and out she came.

She put the tray down by his side. 'I made the biscuits myself,' she told him. 'And I mix the herbs to put in this rich red cordial.'

Biscuits? he thought. *Rich cordial? After such a fine supper?* Then he remembered the old woman's warning.

'You're kind,' he said. 'They'll make the perfect end to a good meal.'

He waited till the princess moved closer to the window to admire the moonlight, then made chewing noises as he slid each biscuit in turn beneath the blanket. After that, he made sipping noises as he tipped the cordial into the plant pot behind him.

Then, guessing why she'd stayed so close to make sure that he cleared his plate and finished the rich red drink of herbs, he yawned and stretched, and let his eyelids flutter as if he had been given some strong drug to make him sleep. 'Such a long walk ... ' he murmured drowsily. '*Such* a long day ... '

Pulling the blankets up more tightly round his shoulders, the soldier closed his eyes.

The eldest princess stood in silence for a while and then she whispered, 'Soldier?'

He lay as if dead to the world.

'Soldier!' she said, more sharply. 'Soldier! Wake up at once!'

The soldier simply rolled away from her and let out a soft snore.

Reaching down, the princess shook his shoulder. He brushed her hand away as if some fly were bothering him in a dream.

To his astonishment, he heard her sigh. 'A shame,' she murmured softly. 'If I did ever marry, I would have chosen a brave, upright man like you. But it turns out that you're as stupid as the rest.' Again she sighed, then ended up more cheerfully, 'Well, never mind. I'll go and cheer myself by dancing the night away along with my sisters.'

The soldier waited till he'd heard her close the bedroom door then sprang to his feet.

'Stupid, indeed!' he said. 'We'll see ... '

He swept up the cloak and threw it round himself. Once he was sure he was invisible, he opened the door a crack and was in time to see the eldest princess kick back a rug and pull at a brass ring set in the floor.

Up came a trapdoor, and one by one the sisters stepped onto the hidden winding stairs and down into darkness.

Hastily, the soldier followed, but the stone steps were so old and uneven that he lost his footing and stepped by mistake onto the trailing train of the youngest princess's dress. She squealed in

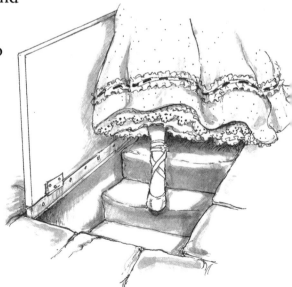

panic, 'Someone has trodden on my gown!'

The eldest sister called back up the line, 'Don't be so silly, dearest. Nobody is behind you. You must have snagged your gown on some sharp stone.'

Down they went – down, down, down – until they stepped out into ancient cellars and on through gloomy caverns. At the far end, there was a gleam of light. The eldest princess walked towards it then pushed at a door, and one by one the sisters hurried out into a silver forest where every twig glistened and every leaf gleamed.

'A silver forest!' breathed the soldier. 'The King won't believe me when I tell him this!' And so that he could bring back proof of what he'd seen, he snapped off the twig end of an overhanging silver branch.

Crack!

The youngest sister spun round. 'What's that? Someone is following!'

The line stopped and the eldest sister said,

'Nonsense, my own beloved! That crack was nothing more than one of our princes firing a salute to welcome us.'

The sisters walked on till they reached a forest of pure gold. Each tree trunk gleamed and each branch glimmered. Every leaf glowed.

'Now this is more than even I can believe!' the soldier told himself. 'So I will take back yet another twig to prove to myself that I was not dreaming.'

He reached up and snapped off the tiniest branch he could see. But even so, it made a noise like a gunshot.

'See!' cried the youngest sister. 'I was right! There *is* someone behind us.'

'Fiddlesticks!' called the eldest down the

line. 'Sweet angel, all you hear is yet another of the princes letting us know they are waiting.'

On they went, till all the golden trees gave way to trees of diamond. Every leaf sparkled. Every twig flashed. Every branch twinkled. The soldier told himself, 'The sisters seem to think nothing of such marvels. But surely the King and Queen will want to know what riches lie beneath their lands.' And reaching out, he snapped off a small diamond branch.

Crack!

Again, the eldest princess calmed her sister's nerves. 'My darling dove, think nothing of the noise. It's just our princes letting us know how impatient they are to see us.'

On they walked, right to the edge of a dark

lake on which bobbed twelve little boats, each with a prince at the oars.

'Come, sisters!' said the eldest princess, and one by one, they stepped into the boats. Seeing no other way to get across the water, the soldier hastily scrambled into the last boat to sit, invisibly, behind the King's youngest daughter.

'How low this boat sits in the water tonight!' she cried out. 'Something is very wrong.'

Her eldest sister's voice rang out to comfort her. 'Don't be a goose, my precious. All that we see is you and your prince in the boat, as usual.'

Across the lake, there was a glorious palace lit by a thousand shimmering lanterns. The boats landed to a fanfare of trumpets and the twelve princes led their partners into a splendid ballroom where they began at once to dance and dance.

The soldier watched for a while, then, knowing that the mystery was solved, he felt an urge to mischief. Creeping up silently behind the eldest daughter as she danced, he seized her by the waist and spun her away from her partner and round the room so fast it seemed to turn into a glittering blur.

First, she was startled. Then, gathering breath just as the soldier spun her back into her partner's arms, she said, 'How speedily you dance tonight!'

The prince, her partner, bowed. The soldier moved on down the line of sisters. But by the time he reached the youngest, he was feeling hot under his cloak, and ready for a deep, refreshing drink. And so, instead of twirling the last sister around as he had all the others, he took the golden goblet she was carrying, drained it to the last drop and hid the cup away under his cloak.

The youngest sister starcd at her empty hand. 'Where did the goblet go? One moment it was in my hand, and now—!' Her tears sprang. 'Oh, why is everything so strange tonight!' But seeing her distress, the eldest sister simply danced past and whispered calmly in her ear, 'My pearl, stop fretting. You must be imagining these things.'

The ball ended only as the first streaks of dawn light lit the eastern skies. The sisters' shoes were worn to ribbons. The princes rowed their partners back across the lake and this time the soldier climbed into the boat that carried the eldest sister and watched how, though she was plainly tired from the hours of dancing, she still smiled and her eyes still shone.

The sisters trailed back through the magic forests till they reached the secret door to the caverns. Here, the soldier hurried ahead through the dark, lonely cellars and made his way up the long, winding stair until he reached the trapdoor. By the time the eldest princess poked her head around the door, he was safely back in his bed.

He kept his eyes closed, knowing she was checking he'd been fast asleep. But then he heard her murmur, 'Oh, what a pity! For I could never marry a man so foolish that he does not realize when he is being tricked.'

The soldier opened one eye. 'Perhaps it was you who has been tricked,' he warned her with a chuckle.

Without a word, the eldest princess swept back into the bedroom, though he could swear that he heard giggling behind the door.

Next morning, the King summoned his daughters. They stood before him in the usual line.

In came the soldier.

'Well?' said the King. 'Have you discovered how my daughters wear their shoes to shreds each night?'

'Indeed I have,' said the soldier, and told the story of the hidden staircase and the marvellous woods, the princes and the lake, the glittering palace, and the great ballroom in which the sisters danced away the night hours.

The King scowled. 'Take your fine tale away with you!' he said. 'The only way I would believe your story is if you had brought back to this palace some sort of proof.'

'Then look at these,' the soldier said, and pulling out the three twigs he had carried back, he held them up to glimmer, glow and sparkle in the morning sun. And while the whole court was so busy staring, he took the golden goblet out from another pocket and winking at the youngest princess, handed it back to her.

The Queen gasped. 'These three short twigs alone amount to great riches. So if the soldier's tale is true, we'll have enough to buy a hundred thousand pairs of dancing shoes, and pay off all our debts!'

'Not *all* your debts,' the soldier reminded her boldly. 'For you and the King did promise me your daughter's hand in marriage.'

He turned to the eldest princess, who stared down at her feet to hide her smile.

'Nonsense!' the King said. 'I must have been so desperate that I took leave of my senses. How can a daughter of mine marry a tattered old soldier like you? No, you must be content with half my kingdom.'

The eldest princess raised her head. 'A promise is a promise,' she declared. 'And I will wed this soldier.'

The Queen was the first to recover. 'He will look fine enough in better clothes,' she admitted.

'And I suppose,' said the King, 'that he has proved to have an excellent brain.'

'That's settled then,' the Queen said. 'And I myself will tell the nannies to burn that dreadful, squalid cloak.'

Before she could stop herself, the eldest princess cried out, 'No one must touch that cloak! For it is magic!'

Astonished, the soldier turned to his new bride-to-be. 'You *knew*? You guessed about the trodden dress? The cracking sounds? The heavily laden boat? The extra dancing twirls? Even the missing goblet?'

The eldest princess laughed. 'Not quite a *guess*. The windowpane beside your little bed shines like a mirror in the moonlight. And I am sure you wouldn't want to marry anyone without the wits to watch you finish the biscuits and drink the cordial.'

'We are a well-matched pair,' the soldier said, laughing, as he kissed her hand. He turned to the King. The King turned to the Queen. The Queen kissed her daughter. 'You shall be married,' she declared, 'and we will hold a ball.

We'll invite all your secret princes. Everyone can dance till dawn, and no one, not even your father, will complain about the cost of shoes.'

So the soldier and the eldest sister were married. And at some busy moment in the middle of the joyous ball that followed, one of the servants saw a little old woman, dressed in black, climbing the palace stairs.

But no one ever saw her coming down again. And in the morning, it turned out the tattered cloak was gone forever.

Diamonds and Toads

Once upon a time, in a far away land that is now well and truly forgotten, there lived a mother and two daughters.

The elder sister was called Drusilla, and she was horrible. She never missed a chance to say a spiteful word and almost everything she did was petty and mean. Why did she act this way? Who knows? Maybe she had been happy and friendly once and then turned jealous when her baby sister Isidora came along. Maybe she was unlucky, with the worst habits of a great-grandfather here, and a great-great-aunt there, all mixed up inside her.

The plain truth was that you would not have liked her if you had lived next door to her and neither would I.

But her mother adored her and thought Drusilla could do no wrong. So when Drusilla quite deliberately trod on little baby Isidora's hand, the mother told herself, 'Drusilla must have tripped!' Or when Drusilla hid Isidora's only precious toy under a blanket at the back of the cupboard in the corner, their mother thought, *Oh, sweet Drusilla! I'm sure that she was only trying to help me tidy the cottage.*

You'd think that Isidora would have grown to be a little wary of her sister, and keep away from her. But quite the opposite. Whenever Isidora saw Drusilla sulking at the bottom of the garden, she'd hurry to sit beside her and ask, 'Sister, what's the matter?'

Drusilla would answer sourly, 'Nothing that someone as stupid as you can make any better!'

Isidora would still beg, 'Please tell me.
I might be able to think of something to
help you.'

And sometimes she did, by doing her sister's
jobs for her, taking Drusilla's turn to search for
the hens' eggs or mending a tear in Drusilla's
pinafore.

One day, when Drusilla was curled in the
armchair, scowling at the empty hearth, Isidora
laid aside her broom and came to her sister's
side. 'Drusilla, you look so unhappy. What's
the matter?'

'Nothing that you can change for the better,'
Drusilla snapped as usual.

'Just tell me,' Isidora begged. 'Maybe I can
help with whatever it is that troubles you.'

'You?' snarled Drusilla. 'How could you help
me? You must know you're the main part of
the problem!'

'What problem?' Isidora asked her, startled.

'We're so miserably poor!' Drusilla cried.
'Mother and I had little enough to spare when

there were just the two of us. But since you
came along as one more mouth to feed, things
have been worse and worse. Why, I've not had
a new dress since the day you were born!'

'Oh, poor Drusilla!' Isidora said, and fretted
and worried till she had a plan. Without a word
to her sister, she went around the village, begging
everyone to give her scraps of cloth from their
rag baskets. 'Any old tattered pieces,' she told
them. 'I can use them all.'

Most of the people in the village were kind,
and searched in their piles of old rags to draw
out a piece of scarlet velvet here or a blue
ribbon there – anything they thought they
could spare. 'Take them,' they told Isidora.
'We'll be delighted if you can use them better
than we can.'

So every night after Isidora had fed the
chickens and swept the cottage floor and washed
the crocks, she'd wait until her mother and sister
were asleep then creep into a corner and stitch
by moonlight till her fingers were sore.

By the time Drusilla's birthday came around, Isidora had sewed the scores of tiny rags together in such fine patterns that the colours shimmered. She held up the dress and told herself, 'It's beautiful! Drusilla will fall in love with it the moment she sees it!'

But in the morning, when she showed it to her sister, her sister snarled, 'Is this all that you have to offer me? A dress made out of rags?' And throwing it into the ashes on the hearth, she turned her back and would not speak to Isidora the live-long day.

Out in the garden, digging up onions and potatoes she had grown to feed her mother and sister, Isidora wept. 'Drusilla hates the dress I spent so many hours making. Maybe the best birthday present I can give my poor sister is to leave home. She and our mother will be much happier without me.'

Next morning, after she had let the restless hens out of their coop as usual, she slipped through the cottage gate and crept away. She walked and walked, down the lane, through the village and into the old forest. She walked for hours until she reached the strangest little forest clearing, unlike any she had seen before. In front of her, on the soft grass, stood an old water well, and leaning over its stone edge was a bent old woman, wearing the shabbiest grey cloak and hood. 'Child,' said the woman, 'be kind enough to reach down and pull up a bucket of water, so I may fill my jug.'

'Gladly,' said Isidora. And though the bucket seemed far heavier than any she had ever come across, she pulled and pulled and pulled on the rope until at last she'd tugged the bucket to the top. She tipped it carefully, filling the bent old woman's jug till the bucket was empty.

'You must be thirsty after your efforts,' the woman said. 'Take a small drink yourself.'

So Isidora took a sip of water and then another. But she had walked for hours and she was hot. Before she knew it, she'd half-drained the jug.

'It doesn't matter,' said the woman. 'The bucket's very heavy and half a jug of water is more than enough for me.'

But Isidora shook her head. And though her arms were aching horribly, she let down the bucket into the well then hauled it up to fill the jug a second time.

'You are a kind, polite and helpful girl,' said the woman. Raising herself to her full height, she threw back her hood and let the cloak drop to show that she was wearing a silver gown and was not nearly as old as she had seemed. 'And I should tell you this is magic water you have drunk.'

'Magic?' said Isidora, and even as she spoke the word, she felt a tiny hard thing spill off her tongue. She watched it fall to the ground, where it lay sparkling in a shaft of sunlight.

'Pick it up,' said the lady. 'And guard it carefully because it is a diamond.'

'A *diamond*?'

As Isidora spoke, a second diamond sprang from between her lips. She stooped to pick them both up.

'But how can—?'

Out fell another!

'But *surely*—?'

Yet another!

The lady smiled. 'Go home. Now, maybe, you will find that you are welcome under your own roof.'

'How did you know that I—?'

More diamonds spilled and Isidora fell silent. Again the lady smiled. And, in a twinkling, she and the magic well vanished from Isidora's sight.

So, full of wonder, Isidora put the diamonds safely into her pocket and retraced her steps back out of the forest, along the lane, through the village and in her own garden gate. She shut the hens safely into their coop for the night as usual and went in the cottage.

'You lazy girl!' cried her mother. 'How dare you sneak off for the day and leave your poor sister and me to make the fires and clean and cook while you go gallivanting around the country?'

'But—' Isidora began. And as before, a diamond fell from her lips onto the cottage floor.

Her mother stooped to snatch it up. 'What's this? A diamond? Where did you steal it?'

'I didn't st—'

Out sprang another diamond. This time Drusilla got to it first and held it up. 'No matter where she stole it! This is treasure indeed!'

Again, Isidora tried to explain. 'The diamonds are not stolen! I went deep in the old forest and ... '

But though they let Isidora tell her story, neither her sister nor her mother bothered to listen properly. They were too busy scrabbling on the floor for the jewels that fell from her lips, gathering them in their aprons. Isidora told the whole tale from start to finish, but all her mother and sister  heard of it was that she'd come across a slender lady dressed in a silver gown beside a stone well in a forest clearing and it was she who cast the magic spell.

Soon Isidora fell asleep after her long and tiring day. And since there were no more diamonds to be gathered, Drusilla pouted. 'I'm older than my sister. So why should she be given such a splendid gift and not myself? I'll go tomorrow to get jewels of my own.'

'A fine idea, my precious,' said her mother, and the two of them sat up till late beside the fire, planning a way to spend the riches Isidora had brought home that day and Drusilla might bring home the next.

Next morning, without a word to her sister, Drusilla set off down the lane. Villagers greeted her as she walked past, but she ignored their nods. 'Soon, I shall live in a great house and not have to bother with plain, stupid people like these,' she muttered to herself.

She snapped at the cows who watched her over the hedges. 'You nosy creatures! Get back to your own business.' And as the sun rose higher, she grumbled to herself, 'I should have waited till Mother had exchanged one of the diamonds for a fine carriage. I shouldn't have to tire myself, walking as far as this.'

She reached the forest. 'Horrid, gloomy place!' She clapped her hands together to frighten the birds. 'Leave off that dreadful racket!'

Finally she reached the clearing. There was the soft grass and the old stone well. But there beside it, instead of the tall lady in the silver gown she was expecting, Drusilla saw only a

bent old woman dressed in the shabbiest grey cloak and hood.

'Child,' said the woman, 'be kind enough to reach down and pull up a bucket of water, so I may fill my jug.'

'I'm not your servant,' snapped Drusilla. 'If you want water, you must get it yourself.' And she sat on the grass and waited for the lady in silver with the gift of magic to appear.

After a while, Drusilla realized that she herself felt thirsty. She reached over the edge of the well to pull up a bucket of water, which strangely seemed as light as air. She dipped in her cupped hands and drank her fill, but then, instead of offering the last of the water to the bent old woman, she let the bucket fall back in the well.

'Child,' said the woman, 'I'll ask you one more time. Will you fetch up some water so that I may drink?'

'The bucket's light enough,' Drusilla told her. 'So there's no reason on earth why you shouldn't pull it up yourself.'

'No reason on earth, perhaps,' replied the woman. And she threw off her cloak and hood so that Drusilla saw her beauty and her silver gown, and knew that she came from a magic place.

Drusilla was livid. 'Oh, you have tricked me into getting no gift from you!'

The lady smiled. 'Oh, you shall have a gift,'

she said. 'You'll have exactly the gift that you deserve.'

And even as Drusilla stared at her, she and the well were gone.

Drusilla stood a moment, not daring to say one word, even softly, to herself. She knew how rude and selfish she had been, and she was sure she'd be punished. She hurried home, not even daring to snarl at the birds or the cows. She ran into the cottage, where her mother and sister were waiting.

'So?' the girls' mother asked Drusilla eagerly. 'Did you meet the wonderful lady?'

Drusilla only nodded.

Seeing the anxious look upon her sister's face, Isidora asked hastily, 'But did you draw up the bucket to give her water?'

Small diamonds pinged onto the floor as she spoke. But Isidora barely noticed them. She was too busy watching her sister shake her head.

Pushing Isidora aside, the mother said to Drusilla, 'So tell me, did the lady give you the same gift as she gave your sister? Answer me quickly!'

Drusilla whispered fearfully, 'I do not know,' and even as she said the words, a toad leaped from her tongue to the floor.

Now tears of horror sprang to Drusilla's eyes, and, guessing what had happened, Isidora wailed through a scattering of diamonds, 'Oh, sister! You should have listened to my story better or waited till I could warn you before you hurried off!'

'How dare you blame me!' shouted Drusilla and as she spoke, a fat, warty toad filled her mouth. Disgusted, she spat it out onto the floor. 'Oh, horrid! Horrid!'

Out fell another, just as big.

All three of them fell silent for a moment. Then the girls' mother turned on Isidora. 'This is your fault! You should have told your story better from the start! See what you've done? You've ruined your sister's life!'

'Get out!' Drusilla shrieked as more toads fell from her lips. 'I can't bear to look at you another minute! Get out! Get out!'

Isidora fled from the house in tears – not for herself, but for her sister who'd been cursed in such a dreadful way. 'I must find the lady at the well,' Isidora wailed to herself. 'I have to make her lift the spell! It's too cruel. Too cruel!'

She ran down the lane, through the village and off towards the forest. But it was evening and the sun was setting fast. The shadows gathered and she lost her way. Was it this path? Or this? She couldn't tell. The darkness settled round her and in the end she sat upon a tree stump and cried and cried as if her heart would break.

Next morning, Isidora woke to find sunlight creeping steadily across the glade. In the distance she heard the sound of hunting horns and drumming hooves. Closer and closer the sounds came, till Isidora could feel the ground trembling beneath her feet and suddenly into the glade burst a fine prancing stallion. It bore the King's son and behind him rode his favourite and most trusted servant.

Seeing a pretty girl sitting forlornly on a tree stump, the prince reined in his horse and asked, kindly enough, 'Who have we here? Are you lost in my father's forest?'

Isidora was not at all sure how to answer.
She hadn't found the clearing with the well the
night before. But she might find it in daylight.
And, if not, she could surely find her own way
home. So was she lost? Or not?

'Come!' said the prince, dismounting. 'I'll
have an answer from you. Yes or no?'

Isidora bent her head low to hide her face.
She whispered, 'No, sir,' as softly as she could,
but still a diamond fell and sparkled at her feet.

'What's this?' The prince stepped forward and knelt to pick up the diamond. 'Strange indeed! Here you sit in your shabby clothes and yet you have a diamond! Are you a thief?'

'No, sir! I'm not!' cried Isidora and this time the prince was close enough to see the diamonds springing from her lips.

'This is a mystery,' the prince declared. 'Or the most splendid magic. Can you explain yourself?'

So while the diamonds spilled, poor Isidora told him all about the lady at the well and how her sister Drusilla had been so jealous of the gift of diamonds that she had hurried off to get a gift for herself. But she had shown such rudeness that her punishment had been to spit out toads. She told the prince how she'd been blamed and driven from the cottage and how, trying to find the magic well again, she'd lost her way.

'Can you want *more*?' he asked, astonished. 'Are you determined to spit out rubies as well?'

'No, no,' she wept. 'I simply want to beg the lady in the silver gown to end the spell that so torments my sister.'

The prince gathered the diamonds that lay around her in the grass and put them safely in his velvet cap. 'I know the very clearing,' he declared, and lifting Isidora onto his horse, he led her there.

They found the lady standing beside the well, dressed in her silver gown. And even through her tears, Isidora couldn't help noticing with pleasure that the King's son didn't tell her to ask the favour herself, in her own words, so that more jewels would fall. He simply told the lady what she'd said.

The lady turned to Isidora. 'But if I take away your sister's gift for spitting toads, you may lose yours for spilling out such precious diamonds.'

'I don't care!' burst out Isidora. 'I never asked for diamonds! All that I wanted was to fetch water for you out of the well!'

The lady smiled. 'Your sister's spell will come to an end as the sun sets tonight,' she told her. 'So let us hope that by then she has learned her lesson well.'

Isidora reached out to clasp her hands and thank her warmly. 'I'll run to comfort my sister with the good news.'

'No,' said the prince and blew his horn to call his servant to him. He handed him the velvet cap. 'Take this to the cottage with the news. And say that in return for all these diamonds, I have taken Isidora.'

He turned to Isidora. 'I ask you now to be my wife. But you are not to answer me, nor say another word till after sunset. I wouldn't have you think I love you only for the jewels that fall from your lips for I consider your good nature a more precious gift than any diamond.'

Gently he lifted her onto his horse again and off they went together. And since the land they lived in was so far away, and now is truly forgotten, nobody knows whether, after the sun had set that night, Isidora still had the gift of diamonds or not.

And, since she and the prince lived happily ever after, nobody cares.

Snow White and Rose Red

Deep in the woods, deeper than you or I have ever been, there was a tiny cottage in which lived a woodcutter and his wife. Their first child was born as the first snows of winter fell. The woodcutter held the new baby close as he gazed out of the window at the blanket of pure white that lay around the cottage.

'She is as fair as the untrodden snow,' he said, 'so we will call her Snow White.'

Their second child was born at the very end of summer. The father held the infant in his arms and turned as the last roses of the year tapped their full crimson heads against the window.

'Her cheeks are as bright as any of these petals,' he said, 'so we shall call her Rose Red.'

The sisters grew, year by year. They both had beauty and good natures, but they were very different. Snow White was shy and thoughtful, with such a gift for stillness that even the most wary forest creatures were happy coming close to where she sat.

Rose Red was as lively as a bouncing ball. She sang and danced her way through every day, climbing to the top of each tree and making dams in the streams. And even after their father sadly died, her spirits soon returned, till she was once again jumping out from behind bushes to startle her sister, and running here and there the whole time they were doing jobs like picking nuts and berries or gathering wood for the fire.

'Oh, take more care,' Snow White would beg. But still Rose Red would run around so merrily she'd spill at least one half of anything she carried. So when they reached the cottage, Snow White would pull her sister behind the two bushes their father had planted – one with white roses for Snow White, the other with scarlet for Rose Red. There, out of sight, Snow White would tip some of her own berries into her sister's basket.

'There,' she would say. 'Now Mother will be no more pleased with me than she is with you.'

'You are my greatest treasures,' declared their mother often. 'Your father would be proud of how you grow so tall and strong and kind and merry.'

The years passed peacefully enough. In summer, Snow White kept the cottage as clean and shiny as a new pin and Rose Red cheered the table with bright jugs of wild flowers.

In winter, they closed the shutters against the howling winds and storms of snow, and banked up the fire.

'A story! Tell us a story!' Rose Red would beg. And in the dancing firelight, their mother would amuse the girls with tales of goblins and witches, of fairy godmothers and talking mice, and handsome princes turned into frogs and ogres by magic spells.

One evening, when the snow lay deep outside, there came a rapping on the door.

The girls' mother broke off the story she was telling them. 'By heaven! I pity any poor traveller out in this fierce cold.' She turned to Snow White. 'Open the door, my darling, and let whoever is knocking in to share our fire.'

So Snow White lifted up the latch and opened the door a crack. In poked the thin black snout of a bear.

In terror, Snow White pushed her hardest at the door. But to her astonishment, the bear spoke.

'Oh, let me in, I beg you. I mean no harm. But I'm half frozen. If I don't find shelter, I shall die.'

Instantly, Rose Red rushed over and pulled
her sister aside. 'Let the poor creature come
in! I couldn't stand to think of him out in the
bitter wind and snow, freezing to death.'

'Mother?' said Snow White. 'May we?'

Their mother, too, had just as soft a heart.
'Yes, my dear. Let the bear in and he may warm
himself beside our fire.'

So in he came. Rose Red found rags to brush the snow and ice from his fur, and Snow White mopped up the puddles he made on the floor. When he was dry enough, they let him sit on the rug. And round him the family sat in nervous silence till Rose Red said suddenly, 'Finish the story, Mother!'

So, not being able to think of any reason to refuse, the mother picked up the fanciful tale she'd been telling. The minutes passed and gradually the bear sank lower on the rug till he was stretched out flat, halfway to asleep. Rose Red slid off her stool and leaned against the nearest mound of his black fur.

'He's like the softest pillow!' she declared.

So, after a few more minutes, Snow White slipped off her own hard stool onto the floor and leaned against his other side. 'His fur smells of cold air and woods.'

'He is a handsome beast,' admitted the mother when the story was done. They left the bear asleep beside the dying embers of the fire and crept to their own beds. But in the morning, when Rose Red woke and had assured herself, 'That was no dream!' and run to find him, he was gone.

That night, he came back and he knocked again. And the next, and the next. And by the time the worst of the winter was over, the three of them had come to expect their giant furry visitor who was so gentle, and let them play on him, and twist their fingers in his fur, and ride him round the room, and make him growl for their amusement.

Spring came. Through melting snow there poked up yellow crocuses and white anemones. The trees dripped steadily. The ground beneath the sisters' feet no longer felt as hard as iron.

One morning the bear told them, 'Don't wait for me tonight. I must be gone.'

Rose Red threw herself at the door to stop him leaving. 'You can't just go away like that.'

'I have to go,' the bear said.

'Why?'

'Because the ground is softening. Soon all the goblins will come up from their dens deep in the earth. They'll roam around the forest, stealing whatever they can find. So I must go and protect the last of my treasures from their thieving grasp.'

Rose Red wanted to scold, 'What treasures can a black bear own? Rotted nuts? Wrinkled berries?' But Snow White laid a finger on her lips to silence her sister and Rose Red said only, 'But you will come back? You won't leave us forever?'

'No, no,' the bear said. 'I'll happily come back when winter comes again.'

'You promise us?'

'On my honour,' said the bear, turning to go. But as he heaved his great bulk through the cottage door, a patch of fur caught on a nail and Snow White saw a flash of gold.

Strange ... she thought. Yet, as the very idea of gold beneath an animal's fur was stuff and nonsense, she became quite sure she had imagined it, so said not a word to her sister. Then, to console themselves for losing the company of their beloved bear for so many months, the sisters ran out into the garden and amused themselves by bouncing the glittering raindrops off all the cobwebs that the spiders had spun between their two freshly-budding rose bushes.

A few days later, Snow White and Rose Red wandered a little further than usual into the woods to gather spring flowers. Suddenly, Rose Red stopped and put her hand on Snow White's arm.

'Look, sister! Over there! What's that?'

Snow White, too, peered between the trees to where something brown and green, with a patch of pure white, was frantically hurling itself up and down, and howling horribly.

Quickly Rose Red set off at a run, calling, 'Hurry, sister!' back over her shoulder. 'Whatever it is, it's in trouble and we must try to save it.'

But when the two of them got close, they
saw it was a goblin and he was in no danger,
just a fearsome temper. 'Don't stand and gawp!'
he snapped. 'Idiot girls! Can't you see that
the end of my precious long white beard has
trapped itself under this log? Do something,
you silly, goggle-eyed fools! And do it now!'

Because the sisters were kind-hearted, they managed to ignore the goblin's rudeness. They pushed and pulled together at the log, but could not move it – no, not the tiniest bit and so the beard stayed stuck fast.

So did the goblin. How he howled and howled. 'You half-witted pair! Are you too stupid to think of anything that will free me?'

At that, Rose Red remembered that she'd slipped her sewing scissors into her pinafore pocket before the two of them set off, to cut the stalks of the flowers. 'Hold still,' she warned the goblin. And before the foul-tempered little creature had even realized what she was doing, she'd snipped off the end of his beard.

Now he was free, the goblin danced with rage. 'My beard! My precious beard! You've ruined it forever!'

'Nonsense,' Rose Red defended herself. 'Beards grow. And anyway, you shouldn't be so vain!'

'I'll be revenged on you!' the goblin screamed.

Rose Red just laughed. Now, even more furious, the goblin screamed at both the sisters so fiercely that Snow White thought it safer to pull Rose Red away. But they looked back as they ran, and both saw the goblin reaching into a cleft of the fallen log to tug out a bag so rotted from the winter storms that pieces of gold were spilling from it out onto the grass.

Rose Red stopped running. From behind a tree, she watched the goblin as he gathered up every last coin and ran off down a different path.

Only a few weeks later, the sisters were strolling together beside a stream when they heard the most horrific screeching noise a short way ahead. Snow White ran forward. There, on the bank, the very same little goblin was hurling his whole body backwards, over and over, to try to stop himself being dragged into the water by a strong fish he had hooked on the end of his line.

'Cut the fish loose!' called out Rose Red. 'Better to do that than be pulled into the stream to drown.'

'Stupid, stupid girl!' shrieked the goblin. 'Can't you see that my beard is tangled in the line?'

Again, the fish pulled with all its might. Again, the goblin hurled himself backwards. Rose Red ran behind and put her arms around him to add her weight to the great tug of war. But still the fish was pulling hard. So once again, Snow White pulled the tiny pair of scissors out from her sister's pocket.

The goblin saw her and went mad. 'You noodle-head! Keep those scissors away from me! Don't you think you've already done far too much damage to my precious beard?'

So Snow White waited. But even with Rose Red adding her strength to that of the goblin, the fish was clearly going to win the battle and drag the two of them into the stream.

'Your beard's important to you,' said Snow White. 'But my dear sister is important to me.' And without asking his permission, she leaned across to use the scissors to snip the mingled beard and line.

Rose Red and the goblin fell backwards and the fish swam free.

'Ninnyhammers! Dunces!' shouted the goblin. 'How dare you! How dare you! My lovely beard's half gone!'

'You should be grateful to us,' Rose Red told him sternly. 'We probably saved your life.'

'Nonsense!' the goblin spat. 'Oh, I shall pay you out for this, don't think I won't!'

Reaching into the rushes, he lifted up a fat little woven bag and stomped off towards the woods in one of his furies.

'Careful!' warned Rose Red. 'Some of the small stones in your bag are spilling.'

'Stones?' The goblin turned, and seeing the scattering of small, pale objects on the grass, he rushed to gather them and throw them back into the woven bag. Then, hugging the rotten burlap closer to his chest to stop more spills, he disappeared between the trees.

Snow White said to her sister, 'Did you see how those little round things gleamed? Could they be pearls? Real pearls?'

Rose Red shook her head. 'I don't care

what they were. I only hope we never see that grumpy, miserable little creature again.'

They did, though, only a few days later.

The sisters had been sent to buy thread and needles in the nearby town. As they came out of the woods onto the rocky moor, they saw an eagle, circling overhead.

'She has her eyes on some small tasty prey,' said Snow White. 'Poor rabbit! Or poor hare.'

But Snow White's guess was wrong because, within a moment, both of them were hearing the same old screeching they had heard before.

Rose Red grinned. 'Him again! What is his problem this time?' Together the sisters ran towards the noise, only to find that the eagle they'd been watching had swooped down to fix her claws into the goblin's jacket and now she was lifting him skyward.

'Help me! Help me!' he shrieked. 'Save me, you foolish featherbrains!'

Rose Red was first to reach him. Grabbing one of his dangling legs, she held on firmly till

Snow White ran up and grasped the other.

Both the girls tugged at the goblin to try and drag him down. The eagle, who was the strongest of them all, fought hard to shake away the sisters and swoop off with her prey. But in the end, the giant bird reckoned there must be easier pickings on the moor, and with one last great flap of her enormous wings, the eagle unhooked her talons from the goblin's jacket, and flew away.

The goblin burned with rage. 'My lovely jacket! Torn to shreds! It's ruined! You girls are hideously careless! You care for nothing! Look at the mess you've made of me, tugging and pulling at my clothes till they are ribbons!'

'Perhaps you would have preferred to be eaten by the eagle?' teased Rose Red.

'Hush yourself, silly girl!' the goblin snapped. He glared at both of them then ran round the nearest rock and picked up a tray of stones that winked rainbow colours in the sunlight. 'Look the other way!' he shouted.

Snow White politely turned her back, but Rose Red spun all the way round and was in time to see the goblin vanish down a narrow gap between two rocks.

'That's where he hides himself and all his treasures,' she told her sister. 'Deep underground, in the dark.'

'If only he would stay there,' Snow White sighed. 'For every time we come across the little fellow, he seems to hate us more.'

Then, realizing they had no time to waste, the two of them ran down onto the path that they had taken before.

The market was busy and it took more time than they expected to get through their errands. But in the end, they found the coloured threads and needles their mother needed. They bought seeds for the garden and stared for a long time at all the pretty trinkets on the market stalls.

'We should set off for home now,' Rose Red warned. 'See the sun getting low? We'll have to hurry to be back before dark.'

Snow White gave one last lingering look at the soft, warm, grey muff she longed to buy for their mother. 'Oh, how I wish we had money to spare!'

'Then marry the goblin!' teased Rose Red. 'He's stolen so many jewels that you could live like a princess.'

Laughing, the two of them set off for home. But when they came close to the place where the goblin had slipped into his den, they both fell silent. Neither wanted that foul-tempered little fellow to realize they were near in case he took the chance to jump out and scream at them all over again.

Quietly they picked their way along the path between the rocks. But suddenly, they saw the goblin. He was crouching by a heap of jewels, admiring them in the last rays of sunlight. They heard him chortle greedily to himself, 'Oh, luscious treasure! Pearls, rubies, diamonds, emeralds! I have them all!'

The precious stones sparkled so brightly that Snow White gasped. Hearing the tiny sound, the goblin turned and saw the sisters standing side by side, watching him gloat over his jewels.

'You wicked, wicked girls!' the goblin shrieked. 'Creeping up! Spying on me! Hoping to steal my treasures! I'll steal you both and bury you in some dark tunnel where you'll never be found!'

Rose Red was about to tell him not to be so foolish when, from behind, she heard a rustle in the bushes, twigs snapping and the deepest growl.

She and her sister spun round and there, lumbering out from the undergrowth, was their own winter bear. How well they knew him! Both would have rushed to greet their old companion and playmate, but the goblin had seized the two of them, each by one arm, and he was holding them fast.

'Here, Bear!' he tempted. 'Why bother to attack me? I'm tiny – less than a mouthful for someone as huge as you! So take these two juicy girls instead. They'll make a proper meal. Take them and eat them!'

At this, the bear began to growl even more fiercely. His teeth were bared and shone so white and sharp that the goblin panicked. Seeing the danger he was in, he hastily let loose the girls and bargained for his life.

'Bear! If I can't persuade you to eat these
foolish sisters then let me offer you a handful
of my sparkling treasures.'

At this, the bear rose on his back legs and growled so fiercely that the rocks around threw back the echo. Then he spoke, just as he had when he came begging for help at the girls' cottage door in those first bitter snows. '*Your* treasures, Goblin? None of those jewels belongs to *you*! As you must well remember, you stole these precious stones from me the day you put me under this cruel spell!'

The goblin turned as pale as ash. 'You!'

Now the bear grasped the goblin between his massive paws. 'Yes, me again. And be warned, Goblin! You can steal treasures from my palace! You can bewitch me! But do not ever think that you can trade the lives of these good sisters for your own freedom! I will not let it happen!' And stepping back, the bear reached out to swipe the goblin with his giant paw.

Down fell the goblin instantly, stone dead.

The sisters stared in wonder. But even as they watched, the bear's furry covering

appeared to wrinkle into folds and fall in silken waves around his feet. Out from the crumpled bearskin there stepped a handsome youth, dressed all in gold.

'This is my own true self,' he told the two of them. 'That hateful goblin from the underworld put such a spell on me that I became the bear you saw. And I had little hope of ever getting back to rights again because he said the curse on me would last as long as his own life.'

Rose Red looked down at the poor, pitiful creature on the ground. 'It was the meanest spell. Still, we must bury him.'

And so they did. And after they had said a prayer over his grave, the youth pressed a handful of the scattered jewels into Snow White's hand. 'Give these to your dear mother as thanks for saving my life through those long, bitter winters.'

Rose Red opened her mouth to say how wonderful it was that now they could go back and buy the soft, warm, grey muff her sister had so longed to buy for their mother.

But Snow White burst into tears. 'How can you do this!' she scolded him. 'How can you send us packing with a few silly jewels? Through all those nights beside the fire, we thought you were our *friend*. We learned to *love* you.' She thrust the precious stones that he  had given her back in his hands. 'Take them! I would give any amount of treasure to have you turn into a bear again if it meant we could pass the time as happily as we did before.'

The youth dropped to his knees. 'Oh, gentle Snow White!' he scolded her in turn. 'Did you believe I wouldn't follow you?
Or that, when I knocked on your door, your mother wouldn't let me in? That would be strange indeed – to let a bear into your cottage and yet refuse a prince.'

'A prince?'

And so he was. They were quite sure of it when he came back with servants and pageboys and a fine carriage to take Snow White and Rose Red back with him to his grand palace.

And there they stayed. The prince married Snow White and, within a year, his merry brother married Rose Red. As soon as their mother saw how happy both the sisters were, she was persuaded she should follow them. The princes themselves came by with spades to dig up the two precious rose bushes, one red, one white, and carry them in triumph to the palace.

There the rose bushes bloomed, along with Snow White, Rose Red and their mother, until the end of all their happy days.